PRAYER

MEDITATION

THE TEACHINGS
OF
THE ARCHANGEL GABRIEL

CHANNELED THROUGH
REVEREND PENNY DONOVAN D.D.
NOVEMBER 23, 1991

APPLESEEDS PUBLISHING   ROSENDALE, NEW YORK

Published by Appleseeds Publishing
P.O. Box 101
Rosendale, New York, 12472-0101

www.gabrielfellowship.org
Email: appleseeds@hvc.rr.com

ISBN # 978-1-932746-00-6

First Printing: January 2003
Second Printing: January 2005

TABLE OF CONTENTS

Preface

On a Sunday afternoon in October 1987 the Archangel Gabriel began channeling through Rev. Penny Donovan and for the next twelve years, ending in December 1999, he taught truths and provided spiritual guidance through evening lectures and all day seminars.

Gabriel conducted over 250 of these sessions, all of which were recorded on audiocassettes. Most of the shorter, two-hour evening lectures have been transcribed from the audiotapes and put into booklets.

Publication of the transcriptions of the all day seminars into books is underway. This book is the first in this series. This topic, Prayer and Meditation, was given by Gabriel on November 23, 1991.

-

Introduction

Reverend Penny Donovan is a psychic who has been a natural medium since childhood. She studied under Reverend Edith S. Wendling at the John Carlson Memorial Institute in Buffalo, New York and was ordained in 1960. Rev. Penny obtained her Doctor of Divinity degree from the Fellowship of the Spirit in Buffalo, New York.

In 1964 she founded the Trinity Temple of the Holy Spirit Church in Albany, New York where she served as pastor for thirty years. To devote more time to writing and to the teachings of Archangel Gabriel, in November 1994 she retired as pastor of Trinity Temple and founded Springwell Metaphysical Studies. . In January 2005 she began a new organization called The Gabriel Fellowship for the preservation, publication, and teaching of Gabriel's lessons.

It was during one of Rev. Penny's regular church services, as she was about to deliver her message, that the Archangel Gabriel come through her and he instead delivered the message. In Rev. Penny's words, "In October of 1987, my life changed very drastically one Sunday. I went to church, as I had done for twenty-three years. As I went into my office to get my Bible and get ready to go up on the podium, I felt very light-headed and dizzy and I thought, "Well, I ate dinner early, maybe I just need some food." The feeling kind of passed as I went out on the podium.

"Before I give my talk, we have a meditation. The last thing I remembered was the meditation. The next thing I remembered was standing there at the lectern with everyone standing up and applauding! I didn't know what had happened. The people were saying, 'Oh, it was wonderful! A teacher came.'

"It was during the next few days that the teacher revealed himself to me as being the Archangel Gabriel. He said, 'I will teach you things and if you will follow and do them, they will change your life for the better.'

That was the beginning of twelve years that he channeled through me teaching truths and providing spiritual guidance. His teachings were simple, loving things. I watched the people in my congregation change, evolve, and grow.

He was challenged many times by more than me and never did he ever lose his temper. He never was anything but loving and kind and he never failed to have an answer to any question that was given to him. He was a very powerful loving force in my life and in the lives of the people who came to hear him over the years."

Gabriel taught for twelve years from October 1987 and to December 1999 through all day seminars and evening lectures usually one to two times a month but sometimes more often than that. Most of his sessions were given in Albany, New York where Rev. Penny lived. However, she did travel to other locations to provide opportunities for Gabriel to present to different audiences. Most of his seminars and lectures were audio taped resulting in over 250 recorded sessions.

Over the years, Gabriel's teachings covered a wide spectrum of spiritual truths ranging from the nature of God and who we are as Spirit to our current level of evolvement and spiritual understanding in this physical dimension. He explained how and why we are here on Earth, our purpose for being here, and what we must do to return Home to our Spirit selves.

He covered many topics such as our levels of consciousness, reincarnation, energy, our egos, the power of our thoughts, negative and positive thinking, unconditional love, forgiveness, and the purpose of the experiences we go through in our lives. His central theme was always for us to *live* our truth through unconditional love and with the knowing that we are truly the Children of God.

As Gabriel had told us, he did end his lessons in December 1999. After he left, Rev. Penny has continued her dedication to service in presenting spiritual truths as she is spiritually guided through her own lectures and seminars and her writings. For those who have had the privilege of knowing her,

Penny is a kind and loving person who through her love of God and desire to be of service has given a gift to the world through her ability and dedication to channel the lessons given by Gabriel and through her continued inspirational leadership.

The Gabriel Fellowship makes available audiocassettes and booklets of Archangel Gabriel and Rev. Penny's seminars and lectures. The organization also conducts regular meetings to support those who seek spiritual guidance and continued expansion of their knowledge and understanding of spiritual truths. It is our desire that you find truths in all these lessons that resonate within you and deeply touch your life.

About This Seminar

In this seminar the Archangel Gabriel teaches us about our communication with God both in our talking to God through prayer and God talking to us through meditation. In the first section, he discusses the nature of prayer and how down through the ages we have lost its true meaning. He states that true prayer is wordless and its only purpose is to unify the Spirit of humankind with the Spirit of the Father.

We often ask, "Why aren't our prayers answered?" Gabriel answers this in his discussion on the key to asking for what we want. He also covers the subject of prayers for the sick in his teaching about the cause of illness and how we should pray for the healing of ourselves and others. He concludes his discussion on prayer with an interpretation of the Lord's Prayer.

Next Gabriel discusses meditation pointing out that prayer is the foundation for meditation. While prayer is our touching into the presence of God, meditation is our allowing God to touch into our lives. He describes the difference between concentration and meditation using as an example Transcendental Meditation's use of a mantra.

He gives many examples of meditation practices in different cultures and of people who have used the power of meditation in their lives to accomplish amazing feats. For those people who do meditate, Gabriel humorously tells how many typically meditate and then gives a description and explanation of true meditation. Finally, he offers guidance for a daily meditation with a procedure that we can follow.

Acknowledgments

This book is the result of the efforts of many people who have graciously and lovingly devoted their time and talents to making this first published book of Gabriel's lessons a reality. First and foremost, recognition and deep appreciation go to Rev. Penny Donovan and Archangel Gabriel without whom this book and lesson would not be possible.

Others who contributed to this effort were Joe Donovan in recording the session on audio tapes; Helen Collesides who did the original transcription; Mary Lee-Civalier, Linda Gilbert, and Vincenza Pentick who did the editing and proof reading; and Joseph Pentick who provided the artwork and graphic design for the book. Finally, but certainly not last, I wish to thank my wife, Arlene, for her support and encouragement to see this project through. To all of these people I am deeply grateful.

Virgil McIntosh
Appleseeds Publishing

SECTION ONE

PRAYER

CHAPTER ONE

WHAT IS PRAYER?

T oday we will learn of prayer. Before I begin, I will say one thing: no prayer is ever a bad prayer; no prayer is ever unheard; and no prayer is ever unanswered. I say this in the beginning because you could misconstrue some of the things I will teach you to mean there is a wrong way to pray. There is no wrong way. There is only a lesser and a greater way, a truer way to pray.

In the early hours of the day we will cover prayer. In the later hours of the day we will cover meditation. I do this for a reason. Without a foundation in prayer, meditation does not "work." Also, this seminar is to be used as a teaching device in times to come and it needs to be divided in two parts.

Prayer is your Spirit longing to feel in its fullness the at-one-ment of you and God. The only purpose of prayer is to unify the Spirit of humankind with the Spirit of the Father. It matters not how you form your words or what you are asking at the moment. *The ultimate goal of all prayer is the unification of the Child with the Father. That is the only purpose of prayer.*

That unification is the only true function of anything that you perceive to be prayer because all else is a shadow, an illusion that satisfies the mind of

17

you, the soul of you, and the physical form of you. But that illusion does not or would not satisfy the Spirit of you.

There is no one who does not pray. Even those who proclaim themselves to be nonbelievers in a higher force pray. Prayer is the connecting link of your life expression with the expression of your Creator. It is the uninterrupted flow between life and Life. It is love seeking to find its own level. It is joy awaiting the ripple of laughter. Prayer, in its totality, is that singular oneness that unites all life in all its forms into the one unit that you call God.

In your descent in consciousness from that at-one-ment that you began with into the state that you allowed yourselves to come down to, you developed many forms of consciousness along the way. You lost a lot of your awareness and you are now on the journey Homeward to rediscover it.

You came from that oneness where you knew that the very expression of your being was a prayer, a prayer of joy. That prayer was the song of eternalness that resonated throughout all of creation; a song that still can be heard this day in your time if you listen with your Spirit.

Prayer is a constant sounding of praise; of acknowledgment from whence you came forth; of a peace that cannot be held, bounded, or in any way disturbed by anything that is not of its truth and of its essence. That prayer has never left you. That type of knowingness is ever present in you this day as it was — I hesitate to say, "back then" because it denotes a passing of time and time is an illusion, but I will say it — back then.

What has happened is, you have put on yourselves many forms of consciousness that have dulled the sound of the song of praise that is the true prayer of the Son of God unto the Father. Because you did that, you perceived that there had to be different ways to pray. You perceived that there are those whose power of prayer is greater than yours, and you perceived — through the eons of time that you have manufactured — that you have needed a mediator to bring your consciousness, your awareness, unto the conscious awareness of the Father.

Because you have believed that, you have created lesser modes of communication with God. It has only been His unending love of you that has caused the channel of true prayer to remain open; for you, left to your own devices, would have closed it long ago.

You are told in your Scriptures "to pray without ceasing." That phrase has been misinterpreted because of the way it was written. There is no creature the Father has created that does not pray without ceasing, for the very existence of you is a form of prayer. And so it is when we say unto you, "pray without ceasing," it means to become aware of the Truth that you, as you are in existence this moment of your time, are a living prayer unto the Father and that prayer in the very existence of you is one of praise.

We will get into the various aspects of prayer that you have created, including their results. But before we do, I want you to be firmly established in your awareness of what prayer really is. Prayer is you. The fact that you are is a song of praise unto the Father. When He called you forth in His intimate knowing and lovingness, He called you forth to join in Him, with Him, in the song that fills the Heaven-world. You, as humankind, are part of a harmonic "symphony," if you will, of sounds that come forth from every living thing.

All of creation has its own tone, its own sound, its own note. Humankind is a singular note, but every human being is a variation of that note. If you were to play that note on an organ or a violin, or an instrument that you blow in, or on each one of your other instruments, you would have that same note, but it would sound different.

Just as you are aware of the various musical tones of your instruments for your note, so the Father is aware of the various musical notes, the harmonies that are the creations that came forth at His bidding.

When you are in tune with that sounding, you have linked into a prayer that has been brought to your awareness. In your awareness you become aware of God, and thusly, know that linking, that joining, that oneness. This unification between the Spirit of you and the God that is, is like a pure bell that tones throughout eternity. All other prayer is lesser than that and while it has its sounding, the sound is less pure and not heard on all levels.

There is nothing the Father is not aware of. However, the importance of prayer is not unto God, but unto yourselves. It is in your awareness that prayer has its importance, for if you are not aware of your prayer, then you perceive your prayer to be unheard. The Father is never unaware of you in any form, from the highest, most sacred moment of your coming forth to all of the lesser things that you dally around in and play with in your illusion.

When you know you have made that ultimate connection with the life in you to the Life that is and you discover they are the same, that is prayer. In your spiral downward in your awareness, you lost the ability of touching into that harmony of the Universe. You lost your conscious awareness of that singular tone, that pure bell-like sounding that emanated from your Spirit. You no longer heard it.

The Father never lost the sound of your tone, but you lost it. In your seeming unawareness of its clarity, its purity, you perceived you were missing something, but you did not know what it was. You could not say, "Ah behold, I am missing the clarity of my prayer with God." So you searched for some way of expressing that clear, pure, harmonic sound.

The next thing you could connect with prayer was chanting. You instinctively knew that what was missing was sound. You knew it had to be something that emanated forth in such purity and beauty as to be beyond even the voice of angels. You sought it and so you came to chanting.

True prayer is without words. Language is one of the most limiting things you can engage in, but chanting is wordless. Chants that have words are limiting and fairly useless for they bring your mind down and lock it into the meaning of a word. Thusly, the purity you are seeking is lost.

But to sing unto God without words, whether it is from the physical throat of you, from the purity of thought of you, or — if you are so fortunate as to have come that far — from the soul of you, it is wordless. It is a sound to your ears only that repeats what is in your memory from way back — the clear, pure sound of you and God at one-ment. That is prayer!

CHAPTER TWO

ASKING THE FATHER IN PRAYER

There was a time upon your Earth when you had no languages. You simply used body language, grunts, groans, gestures. It was quite interesting to walk among you at that time. You sounded like a pen of those little creatures with the curly tails. By this time, you had also lost touch with the idea there was a singular God and you had created for yourselves all these gods of thunder, lightning, the ocean, etc.

When you created language, one of the first things you discovered was one of the biggest illusions that you perpetrated throughout your generations. That was the idea that you could ask God for something. In your states of consciousness in prayer, you went from chanting to asking. Have you ever heard anything so ridiculous in your life — to ask God for something? It is like taking a mouthful of water and asking the water to quench your thirst. What else would it do?

Do you think that you need to ask the Father for anything? Do you think that He is so totally unaware of you that He is not aware of your every aspect, including the illusion of lack that you perpetrate upon your Earth? I can see all the wheels turning, "But I thought we were supposed to come to God and ask Him for what we wanted."

What happens when you ask for something? It implies a lack of it, does it not? When you ask for something, you are implying that you do not already have it. Therefore, you are depending on an outside source to bring it to you because you, yourself, do not have it. This is one of the biggest ways to separate yourself from the Father. When you perceive you are lacking something and you ask the Father to give it unto you, you have already closed the door to receiving it.

The True Way to Ask

As you progressed in your states of consciousness in prayer, you went from chanting to asking. Chanting was a purely worshipful type of prayer. It was not asking for anything. It was simply acknowledging the presence of and being joyful in the gods you believed in.

The true way to ask is to come into the consciousness of the acceptance of that which you desire. For when you ask in an attitude of lack, your prayer will be answered in an attitude of lack. This is how you get such limited blessings. When you perceive yourself to be lacking in something, it is because you have not lifted your consciousness to the awareness that you already have it. Therefore, when you ask in an attitude of lack, you are saying to the universe, "There is only one of —" or "I only need this." What you are doing is taking a crumb instead of the loaf.

In your Scriptures there is a parable of a woman who approached the Master Jesus and asked if she might learn from him. He said, "It is not meant to feed unto dogs that which is for men," and she said, "But if I could have but a crumb from under your table, I will be filled." That was the correct answer for her to give. If you read that parable in its literal sense, it appears the Master was casting her away because she was a woman, or for whatever reason, and that he did not deem her worthy to hear his words. Is that not how it would appear unto you?

But what he was in effect saying to her was, "You would not understand my words until you lift your consciousness up to where you can accept that which is already here for you." Her response, "If I could have the crumbs under your table," told him where her consciousness was; that she felt life was doled out in little tiny pieces and that she had never experienced the fullness of life. None of you here have either. You are all under the table looking for crumbs. I am here to give you a loaf, or ten loaves, if it be your pleasure!

What do you do when you are in a state of lack in your consciousness, when you lack something, and you ask of God? If I am standing here telling you that it is not a good thing to ask God, not a correct thing to do, then what does one do when one perceives there to be a lack of something in one's life? Go back to the resounding tone, that pure, clear, harmonic sound that is you and the Father being one.

Oh yes, you can. I hear all your thoughts, "I don't know how to do that. I can't do that." You can because you do it all the time, only you just don't know you are doing it. When you lift your awareness to the highest level you are capable of at this point in your evolution, there is an aspect of your Spirit that touches into that clear bell-like silver tone. Even though you are not consciously aware, there is a silver sliver of it permeating down through the many layers of consciousness you have created, down into your consciousness to spear your heart into awareness.

Are you familiar with the picture in the Catholic churches that is called the "Sacred Heart of Jesus"? It is a picture of the Master Jesus with his heart exposed, a little slice in it with little drops of blood coming down. Do you know what the true meaning of that picture is, what it is out-picturing, and whence it came forth? It came to one of the brothers in a vision and he misinterpreted the vision. It represents that sliver of clarity of the true prayer of the Spirit of you in its unification with God that reaches down and pierces the heart of you unto awakening.

The blood that came forth represents the issues of life you perceive yourselves to be captured in. It is the bleeding away of the illusion, the dream you created, to allow the pure truth of your being to be brought into your awareness. That is the meaning of that picture. Everybody always thought it was because he was sorrowful for all the nasty things you were doing, isn't that true?

The Key to Asking for Something

The key to asking for something you desire is not as complicated as it would appear. First of all, the fact that you desire it is the awakening within you of the idea that you already have it. So what would appear in your perceptions to be lack are really the birth pains of the fulfillment of it; for if you did not desire it, you would not call it unto yourself.

Know you the billions of things you allow to pass you by every moment of your existence because you have not called them forth? They simply go on past you; streams of them go on past you! When you perceive you have a need, it is that aspect of your inner-self that is aware of the fulfillment and is drawing it to you.

Where you get confused is you get locked into the

idea of the don't-haves. You perceive something as being absent instead of perceiving it as being on its way to manifestation to you. If you are unaware of it, how could you desire it? You couldn't. You wouldn't know enough to. So the very fact that you desire something is the calling of it to you to be made manifest in your life.

When you perceive a lack, instead of going to the Father and saying, "Pleeez let me have . . . !" — Oh, you all do it! — you would say unto the Father, "I rejoice in Your presence that You have brought to my attention this wondrous blessing that is manifesting for me and I thank You for it." And you become joyful in it! I promise you, it will materialize for you.

What happens when you perceive a need is that you get locked into the need aspect and do not go past it, so the need keeps repeating and repeating and repeating, and all you get is need.

CHAPTER THREE

THE CONSCIOUSNESS OF LACK

You must realize that abundance comes from the spiritual connectedness between you and the Father. If you ask only for an object or a thing, you are asking for the thing to bring itself to you. Now, I can see your confusion. I want to go back to the states of consciousness. An attitude of lack is, in its truth, the closing of the door to blessings.

Let us suppose a wealthy relative passes into the Spirit world and leaves you a grand and glorious mansion with a thousand rooms filled with a thousand glories! You enter the entryway, you behold all of it, and you shout, "Ah, indeed, this is wondrous! I will make my abode here." You settle yourself in the entryway and you never go any further.

Now comes "potty-time" and there is no bathroom in the entryway! Now you perceive yourself with a lack, do you not? What happens is you are in this room without the facilities you require for your bodily functions. So there you sit and you say, "Dear Lord, please let me have a bathroom!" and you look about you and behold, there is none! So, you pray all the more earnestly until finally you are driven from that room to find yourself a bathroom!

This allegory is what you do when you pray for some thing. You have not allowed yourself to become aware that somewhere out there is a bathroom awaiting your arrival through your consciousness. Here you have this abode of a thousand rooms filled with all its glory, but if you take up residence in one room only, that one room is not going to have everything that you desire or perceive that you need, is it? So you must explore other areas of consciousness. Each room is a state of awareness in which you become aware of what is in that room.

When you perceive you need to take a certain action and you are not clear what that action might be, but you want it to be the right one, in your awareness lift yourself into the next state of consciousness. You can do this. It is a matter of closing your eyes and bringing yourself up. You affirm, "I have the correct action. That which I am about to do is it!" And, it will be.

If you ponder it, if you worry about it, if you dwell upon it in a negative way, "If I do this, then so-and-so is going to do that and that's not going to bring any good consequences," if you do that, you are going to lock yourself into the need and not into the action.

You can ask the angels for help. When the angels came to Earth in a recognized form — before humankind decided they were beyond that nonsense

— angels came with a specific "duty," as it were. One of the things they did was to herald that tone that I discussed earlier and bring it into the resonance of the cells of people. There are angels called the Angels of Destruction and one of the things they do is remove the barriers of awareness.

When you perceive a lack, whether it is lack of health, lack of funds, or lack of love, it is because you are perceiving something is missing. Actually, what you desire is there, but your eyes are veiled; you do not see it; you are not aware of it.

When you call on the Angels of Destruction to come and remove the veils, that is all they do. They take away the blindness of your spiritual eyes and allow you to see. They unplug your ears and allow you to hear. They gather up your wounded emotional body and comfort it. They take off the painful garments that you have placed thereon and they allow that child of your feeling nature to kick its feet, experience its nakedness, and rejoice!

Praying yourself out of an attitude of lack is very simple. Yet, it is something that requires great diligence, for the ego of you would have you believe in lack because this is one of the ways it controls you. It keeps your senses keenly tuned to what you don't have. That is one of the ego's greatest ploys. It uses this right unto your death. When you take your awareness out of that room of lack and allow it to explore the avenues of your own spirituality, you will find an answer to everything.

No matter what you are praying for, no matter how you are praying, it comes to this, beloveds — there is only one prayer. That prayer is the unification of your Spirit with the Father God. All of these other things you perceive yourselves needing, requiring, desiring, are only the illusions you have of yourselves as being less than the Children of God.

Tell me: What other prayer could there be of any importance, other than the unification in your consciousness of your at-one-ment with God? Is there another that would have that importance? Is there another that would bring you peace? Is there another that would cause you to be so loved? Is there another that would give you wisdom? Is there another that would ever satisfy the craving of your Spirit to go home?

The toys you have upon your plane of illusion are so valuable to you. Tell me, beloveds, how long will the joy of possessing them comfort you? How long will the love you pour out on them sustain you? How long will it be before you find a restlessness within you, a boredom with them, a disinterest, a lack of caring? How long will it be before the Spirit of you tires of dallying with them and longs to feel for more than what you have? How long will it be before you are out searching for more toys and more illusions and more dreams to satisfy the craving within? When one prayer, one answer, is the answer to it all!

For if you have God, and you *know* you have God, are not all other things added unto it? Are not the toys of your world given unto you from a Father who revels in your joy and would give unto you all things, whatever you desire, to hear your laughter, to see your smile, to feel your warm embrace of acceptance of His gifts unto you?

"Seek ye first the kingdom of Heaven," which is your knowingness. It is that clear-sounding silver tone throughout the universes that says, "One more Spirit Child has returned in knowingness unto the Father." All these things, these lesser things, these temporal things, these play-by-the-wayside things, will be added unto you and you will be allowed to play your games of whatever you choose for as long as you like in perfect peace. But it is in the finding of that clear note, that one singular prayer that is *all* prayer, and indeed the *only* prayer there is that says, "I'm coming home, Father! Put the light in the window for me."

CHAPTER FOUR

PRAYERS FOR HEALING

W hat about prayers for physical well-being? Is there anybody here who has not had a need for that at one time or another? What is the prayer for physical well-being? Now think before you answer. When you pray for yourself or for a loved one to be made whole and well again in the physical form, from what source does your request come? Your request is based on the false god of fear.

I can hear everybody saying, "But that's not true. I want him to be well." Indeed and why do you want him to be well? Isn't it because you fear he will pass away out of your physical sight? You fear that his pain and anguish will disturb your sense of peace? You fear that he will not enjoy life in its fullness. You fear that he will not remain upon the earth. You fear, you fear, you fear.

What is Illness?

I will tell you how to pray for healing, for there is a true prayer for healing. I have told you that you need to give only one healing and that is true. I will tell you how that one healing comes about on the spiritual planes.

Illness in any form is one of the biggest illusions. It is based only on fear and it is the wildest creation of the ego. I will tell you why. You are perfect, absolutely perfect. Everybody thinks that illness produces discomfort, worry, pain, suffering, death. It doesn't. Those are the results, not the cause. The cause of all illness is the desire to punish the wayward Child of God and cause that Child to suffer for his "sins."

I don't care whether you have a tooth that bothers you in the middle of the night, a cancer, or a heart "attack," as you call it. Your heart has never attacked you, but that's what you decided to name it. It doesn't matter, an accident or anything that seeks to harm the physical form is a tool of the ego. The ego uses this quite freely because how else could the ego remind you how vulnerable you are, how temporary you are, and how you must cling to life or you will die. You know that death is forever! Right?

So when you pray for healing out of fear, guess what you are going to get back? Illness, indeed! That illness may not manifest in the same form again, but it will reappear in some way.

Healing and Forgiveness

Healing has to come from the Spirit of the person experiencing the perceived illness. Another can send healing to him, but until he accepts it, it will not manifest perfect health.

When you can forgive yourself for what you perceive to be worthy of punishment, you will be perfectly healthy. Your idea of punishment goes back to the idea of drifting away from God. It goes back to the time when you first perceived that you and God were separate. I said "perceived" because if you knew what you were doing, you would have known better. But you perceived yourself to be separate and this perception is also the basis for your idea of asking God for something "out there," when in truth it comes from within.

Your perception of illnesses goes back to the idea of being punished. The early Church Fathers were great ones for perpetrating the idea of hell, damnation, being cast into hell with Satan and all his angels.

I want to give you a little allegory. Suppose you take a group of little children and put them in a big room with all kinds of things such as toys, furniture, and books and you don't supervise them. You sort of let them go about on their own. Then one of the children breaks something and you walk in the room. Have you ever noticed that nobody in there did it?

Well, you sort of do the reverse. God gave you creation to play in and as soon as you perceive there is something wrong, you all decide that you did it. You and your neighbor, their neighbor and so forth, the whole lot of you are guilty, right?

What happens when little children do something they shouldn't? Do they not have to sit in a corner or get their bottoms patted or whatever it is you do? Is there not some form of retribution that you take against these little ones for having broken something or for whatever they did? Now that is your concept of what God does.

Somebody created mosquitoes and God has been after him ever since! Somebody created disease, death, and torment, so somebody has to pay for all that, is that not true? That's what you think God thinks? How else would you have come up with the Law of Karma and the Wheel of Karma? Do you think God created that? God wouldn't know karma if He found it in His sandal!

Karma was your idea. What a wondrous way to punish yourselves! You took the perfectly good Law of Cause and Effect and you twisted it around to suit your idea of being punished for something you think you did that you shouldn't have. So you decided, "If I do this to so-and-so in this lifetime, the next lifetime he can do thus-and-such back to me," and you could go on like that forever, and you have. You have been constantly paying debts.

On that theme of debts, is there anybody in this room who does not have debts or not owe anybody money? Everybody owes somebody something. Is that not the most wondrous out-picturing of the Law of Karma that you have ever seen in your lives? Everybody is in debt to somebody somewhere! Where do you think that idea came from? Do you think that when the Father created a rose, He asked the lilac bush to "put it on the tab"?

Think about it, beloveds. How many of you here feel you do not owe anything? How many of you here feel you have the right to come back to the earth plane because you want to, desire to, and not because you owe somebody something from way back when? Many of you feel you are going to have to come back to pay for your "sins," do you not?

Perfect Health and Dying

The prayer for perfect health begins with the recognition that it is your natural heritage. The physical form you created in which to manifest on the earth plane has the right to perfect health. There is no reason why any of you here, if you choose to die, cannot die in perfect health. The body does not have to have an illness for you to leave it behind. That's another myth. Every day there are thousands of people all over your Earth plane who die in perfect health. There is no reason why anyone cannot, if he chooses to do so. If you choose to take your body with you — that's another story — you can still do that in perfect health.

Let's assume you decide to hang onto the illusion of death unto the point where you practice it. You do not have to die of some malady. You can simply choose to lay aside the physical form and go on. People do it all the time. The Native Americans have that down pat; so do many of the Aborigines around the earth. That is a perfectly natural out-picturing of your desire to leave the earth plane without harming the vehicle that served you so well while you were here upon the earth. Actually, the body has the right to never know pain or distress of any kind. After all, you called it forth to serve you and it served you very well. If it is not serving you well, guess whom you need to have a talk with? Yourselves.

How to Pray for Healing

Prayers for healing start with the recognition that you are Spirit. In that spirituality you are heirs to everything that is good, holy, and sacred. You have the ability to manifest that holiness down through all the states of consciousness that you have, down into the physical form. The cells of your body are programmed for perfect health, everything about you radiates the Father, and the Father is perfection.

40

When you pray only for healing a particular malady, you are not praying for the whole person. If you pray not to have a certain ailment, you are not considering the rest of you: the rest of your physical form, the rest of your mental abilities, the rest of your emotions, the rest of you as a total person. Praying only to be healed of a certain disease is like climbing under the table looking for crumbs when there is a whole loaf on the top of the table. Asking to be made whole includes every aspect of your being and that includes becoming aware of the resounding of the spiritual tone, that silver bell-like resonance that is the at-one-ment of you and the Father.

CHAPTER FIVE

THE LORD'S PRAYER

Repetitious prayer is a binding thing and it locks you in. You do not need to repeat unto God anything. He hears you the first time around. People who pray the same prayer over and over are only saying words. The words are heavy for there is no love in them and so they are not light and very rarely travel very far from the person speaking them.

When you pray in fear, your words strike against a wall and fall back unto you. When you pray with power, there is no wall that can contain your feelings. Any prayer that does not have feeling in it is better off not to be prayed, for it goes nowhere.

You have the Lord's Prayer which contains within it the affirmation of every good that the human Spirit could actually desire while encased in the flesh. The essence of this prayer is to make you aware, if you will think on its words.

Our Father, all life, none exempt, all collected. Our Father, the Creator, we recognize You *who art in Heaven*, the state of absolute perfection that is within the human Spirit; the "Divine Essence," as it were, out-pictured.

Holy is Your name and in Your Holiness so are we

made sacred; the unification of Child and Parent.

Thy Kingdom, the kingdom of the Spirit, which is all kingdoms, ***come*** forth upon this the lowest, the thickest, the heaviest sphere, the earth in the fullness that is there in the Heaven-world.

Give us this day, allow our awareness to be opened, ***our daily bread*** which is the Spirit of you in the at-one-ment of God. That is true bread; it feeds you; it is your life substance.

Forgive us our trespasses while we are yet in a mode of consciousness that we believe we need to be forgiven. Help us to go past that point at which we understand we have sinned and lead us into the light of our awareness in which we know we have never sinned.

And in this ***we have forgiven*** our enemies or ***those*** we perceive to ***have trespassed against us***. For every enemy that you perceive out there is only the "enemy of the within" that you think you have. There are no outside enemies, beloveds. They are all the illusions that you have internalized and claimed to be your own. They are the empty dreams, the shadow land, the lifelessness that you perceive to be truth.

It is the emptying away of that illusion as you say, ***"Forgive us our debts, as we forgive our debtors."*** There are no debts.

Lead us not into the temptation of believing in the ego-self, *but deliver us from the evil* of our own creative thought in which we perceive that we can be ill or die or in a state of lack.

For Thine is the Kingdom. What other Kingdom is there, beloveds? Thine is the Kingdom upon Earth, upon any plane.

And the **Power**. What power is there excepting the power of the Divine? What power could there be excepting that of God, for there can be none like unto Him?

And the Glory. Can there be glory beyond God? Your glory is the glory of the Father shining through you.

Forever. Indeed! You are in forever now. Ever have you been and ever will you be.

So this prayer is the affirming of all that you require while on the earth. It satisfies every outward need and comforts the internal self. However you pray, pray with the knowingness of the connectedness of you and the Father. Never use God's name to curse or damn. Never call upon the Most High to strike down or to curse anything, for you call on a myth — for God cannot destroy.

CHAPTER SIX

SUMMARY OF PRAYER

When you pray for another, whatever that prayer is for, you are praying for you, for what happens to one happens to all. When you ask God to bless another, you are asking, in effect, that his awareness be awakened unto the blessings that the Father has already given him. And in asking for his awakened state, you ask for your own. Whatever you pray for another, you pray also for yourself. Whatever you ask for yourself, you ask for another. Ever have I said there is but one prayer.

Because you have taken unto yourselves the many veils of consciousness and have perceived lack, illness, death, and all manner of negative things, you have beset yourselves with the task of praying yourselves out of those conditions. In truth, you only need to let go of the dream and reach for the Light. You will find that you do not need to pray yourself out of anything. The only thing that binds or imprisons you is your own unwillingness to see past the prison walls. Once you have seen past the walls, nothing can ever bind you again.

Prison walls take many forms, beloveds. You have all built your own prisons. Some of you perceive your prison to be in the action of another; some of you perceive it to be in illness; and some of you perceive it to be in the taking away of something you have loved. But all of these things are only the ego telling you a lie.

Look past your prison walls and behold the Christ set free, the Son of God unfettered. Listen to the angel wings that flutter past you, humming the echo of your song, your note, your clear bell-like tone that is you and the Father in prayer. How limited in your sight and hearing you are when you listen to the physical world! You are so much more than anything your five senses teach you — so much more!

Each time I come I peel away another layer. You are all like onions with little thin skins that I peel away! I watch the glimmers of light glow brighter around you and in you, and I know that you have learned yet another and another and another lesson that lifts you always ever into the Light.

You are beauteous! Wondrous! And I am privileged to come and to serve you. One day, we will all gather together and see each other for what we really are and say, "Ah behold, I had no idea you were so beauteous, indeed! Had I ever known, I would have followed you home!"

I trust that what I have said to you today has been understood. It has been one of the most difficult assignments, to teach you prayer, because prayer has been so misconstrued throughout your generations.

Have you any questions to ask on prayer?

CHAPTER SEVEN

QUESTIONS ON PRAYER

Raising Ourselves into Light

Participant: When you refer to raising ourselves into the Light, I see my physical being raised above the earth, the planets, the sun, the universe. Do you mean raising our consciousness in any other way?

Gabriel: Whatever you can create in your mind that will give you sense of at-one-ment with the Father is all right to use. But it is the feeling of it as well as the visualization. For you can visualize anything, but if you do not feel that connectedness, you are still keeping it out there. You are not allowing it to be internalized.

Whenever you are envisioning yourself connecting with God, it is important to feel that connectedness. Let it become your reality. It is not far away from you. You perceive yourselves to be distant from it. Indeed not, it is closer than your breathing. It is a matter of allowing the other senses of you to fall away until there is just that one sense within you.

A Sense of Oneness and True Prayer

Participant: You were talking about our getting to that one sense of at-one-ment with God in our prayers. Does that one sense give us the feeling of our other senses falling away such as outside noises, itching, scratching, our minds wandering, and other things of that nature when we pray?

Gabriel: You would not be aware of them, Beloved Woman. When you are aware of your physical body in prayer, you are not truly praying. True prayer transcends the physical, the mental, and the emotional. True prayer is when you recognize that the physical aspect of you is a prison, a cell, a room — the singular room that you went into in your great abode — and that you have passed through that room.

True prayer is when the mind of you no longer thinks thoughts that are distressing to you or calls your attention away to something else. It is when you have passed that room. True prayer is when your feeling nature leaves behind all of the illusion of pain, disappointment, doubts, and fears. It is when the feeling nature of you is aware of only one feeling, your at-one-ment with God and the unity of that moment in which you and the Father are one. You know it because you feel it. It is a feeling.

It matters not what you have visualized. It matters not where you have been in your consciousness because true prayer will transcend all of that and allow you to be aware of that unification. That is what happens when you pray from the very Spirit of you. You bring the songs, the chants, up into the harmonic sound of that one clear note that you are.

Being in Prayer While at Work

Participant: What I understood from what you said earlier was that I could be in prayer in doing everyday things. I could be unifying myself, my Spirit, with the Father God just in the expression of how I am being at the moment. Then you just said that true prayer transcends the mental, the emotional, and the physical. Does that mean that when I am in my everyday conscious level of doing my work that involves the mental and the physical, I have then cancelled out the prayer I thought I understood earlier?

Gabriel: No, you have not "cancelled it out," as it were. When I said your very existence was a prayer unto the Father, this is a truth. As you go about your tasks, whatever they are, you are aware of the presence of the Father and in that awareness everything you do is brought unto Him.

In the olden days, people came and brought their gifts unto the altar of God. They laid thereon their little creatures, their baskets of grain, and so forth. When you are attuned to that silver clarity, that note that is you, and you are upon the earth with tasks that cry unto you to be cared for, as you take these, your "gifts," as it were, and present them unto the Altar of God, the echo of that sound that is you — your prayer — embraces that which you are doing, "includes it," gathers it unto itself, and transforms it by the sounding of that which is your prayer. Your task is transformed and becomes sacred.

Prayer is the sounding of that voice of the Child unto God, the parent. It is that sound that is the bell clarity, the harmony, the silver tone that goes out unto limitlessness, eternity. It is a transforming sound; for once having been heard, it is never, ever, forgotten. And having experienced that sound within the very fiber of your being, it transforms the mental body of you and takes it out of its doubt, out of its turmoil, out of its confusion, and brings it into the knowing. The intellect is aroused, touched, and transformed. The thoughts that are coming to you are no longer beleaguered, but rather come in their clarity to you as pure ideas.

This sound then touches and resonates through the feeling nature of you, which is the love of God brought into "form." It transforms your emotional body and brings it up out of its emotions into its feeling nature so that what you feel is the pure love of God which you then recognize as *your* love for whatever and whomever. In that recognition you gather the love of others, of the world, and of God who pours it forth through all creation. You gather it and it is pulled to you. It is wrapped around you and you are loved.

This love cannot be held by you or contained unto only yourself, for love is limitless and it will flow out without any effort on your part. It will go through you, out into your world, and touch into that note which is in all people everywhere around your world. You become that instrument of love and everything you do — it matters not if it is holding a child or sweeping your floor — is love out-pictured. It will be felt, it will be known, and it will be taken in.

Love then comes into the physical form and touches into the cells of your body and transforms all. "Perfect love casteth out fear," so the cells of your form that have been programmed into fear of illness and fear of death are transformed. They are no longer held in bondage unto it and you now are perfect health. You do not *have* perfect health, you *are* perfect health. Then you are perfect love and perfect mind, for this note with its silver spear has pierced all the veils of your being and you have become that which you ever have been.

Participant: I think I understand about being prayer. Is it correct that when we love what we are doing, we are just being and we don't have to know this is prayer?

Gabriel: You know it because it is that pureness that you will not cast off. You cannot not know it. You cannot not feel it. You are aware. This is how everything you do becomes a prayer.

When to Pray

Participant: When we do this prayer, can it be in our awakened state or can it be in our sleeping state?

Gabriel: It can be either.

Participant: Just before we go to bed, could we ask or say for whatever and have this be part of our dream state?

Gabriel: You can do that.

Asking in Prayer

Participant: Can we review the asking part again? You said we are not supposed to ask.

Gabriel: Oh no, I didn't say you weren't supposed to.

Participant: I thought you said if we asked for something, then we were acknowledging a need.

Gabriel: You are. However, in your asking you are also bringing to your awareness your ability to have, and therefore, to accept that blessing into your life. You already have it or you wouldn't be asking for it. So, instead of asking the Father to give it to you, you can say, "Father, I await for You to remove from me the obstacles so that I might be aware of this Thy precious gift to me." Ask to be made aware of what you desire rather than having it placed before you. Ask that you be made aware of the gift. It's that simple.

Participant: Can we ask to be made aware of it, *soon*? I mean, if there's no time on the other side and if we have it right now, then couldn't we be made aware of it now?

Gabriel: Do you think God needs time to think about your request?

Participant: No, I don't. It's our lack of recognition then. So when I say, "Could You please remove it soon," you are saying I should ask God, "Can I appreciate it as soon as possible?" I'm not asking God to do something in that case.

Gabriel: Beloved Woman, there is no such thing as "as soon as possible" with the Father. The moment you are aware of your desire, it is already granted. You are thinking in terms of consecutive events: you ask here; He thinks about it here; He makes up His mind here; He tells someone, "Go take care of it," there; and then you receive it down here!

Instead, it is like this: "Let me be aware —," there it is! Now if you allow your ego to say, "It isn't here. Look about! Do you see it?" then you are in trouble. When your ego says, "It didn't happen, did it? I told you so!" you say to ego, "Get thee behind me. I have no part of you for the Father will bring unto the Son every gift." And every gift is brought in one gift — the awareness of the Son of the Father's love and all things shall be added unto you.

The Bell-Like Tone

Participant: You talked about a tone, a sound. There is a group of people who meditate who talk about the fact that you can learn a specific tone or a sound. They call it a mantra. If you learn that sound and meditate with that sound, then you are immediately in tune with the universe. It appears, after what you said, that they are "off the mark" a bit.

Gabriel: A bit. Their intention is good. But only you can know your sound. Another could not give it unto you. I could not give it unto you. If I could, I would. But the very sound of it is particular to your Spirit. I could not, would not, presume to know the intimacy between you and your Father.

Participant: But you know your sound?

Gabriel: Oh, indeed! Angels, humans, animal life, plant life, whatever, whether it is in the other worlds or in your world, each has its own tone. Do you know how a wild creature will know its own mother among hundreds of other mothers? The wild babies just know their mother.

It is that knowingness, that feeling, that hearing on a level beyond your physical ears of that sound. You know when you are in tune. It is not in the physical ears. There is no physical sound that you could make that would be like it.

Praying for Others

Participant: You said that when we pray for ourselves, it raises everybody up. And when we pray for loved ones, it raises us up too.

Gabriel: Oh, indeed.

Participant: Is there a special way we should pray for relatives? I have a lot of relatives. Is it the same if we say "siblings and children and grandchildren?" Should we name them individually?

Gabriel: A good way to pray for others, Beloved Woman, is to see them as God sees them — as perfect Light in every way. That is the most profound and powerful prayer you can offer on their behalf. You could say to the Christ in them, "I see you as the Son of God, perfect in every way." That's all you need to say.

Healing

Participant: You taught us that children who come into the world with diseases are usually teaching the parents a lesson. Can the parents pray for the healing of a child when the child is sick like that and heal them?

Gabriel: Of course, but their prayer would be more effective if they prayed for their own understanding to be opened so that they could accept the perfect health of this child. Most parents who have a child with a serious or terminal illness are there to learn a lesson in patience and also in the acceptance of the good — not the acceptance of death or of illness — but acceptance of the good. As soon as they accept that good, the child recovers or goes into Spirit, whichever the soul has decided it will do.

Some decide to take the healing in the form of death; others decide to take it in the form of getting better, but either way, it is a healing. Death is the letting go of a form that can no longer serve you. It is allowing the body to go to rest somewhere while the soul is free.

People Who do not Pray

Participant: You said there are none who do not pray. If somebody says he is an atheist or an agnostic, what things does he do that might be interpreted as prayer that he doesn't see as prayer, or is it a subconscious prayer?

Gabriel: The fact that he exists. You know you are a human being. There is no one who could convince you that you are a donkey. It is that same knowingness that is the sounding that is prayer between you and God.

Now, those who claim they do not pray because they do not believe there is anything else, on some level — even as you have in the cells of your body the knowingness to create a physical form that will be human, not a donkey — there is within the Spirit of that individual that "homing device," that toning that he would recognize, that he would hear on some level. Whether he physically admits to it or not doesn't change the fact that the toning is happening and he reacts to it.

Participant: Is there a way to get someone to have that awareness?

Gabriel: No, because it has to come from the within of him. You cannot teach it to another anymore than I can make you aware of your tone, your sound. It is something that is innate. It is in the very fiber of his being.

Participant: So, if you are talking to someone who doesn't believe in anything greater than himself, then that's just where he is.

Gabriel: That is where he makes believe he is. This is all right. He consciously truly believes that there is nothing more at the moment, but that doesn't make it true.

Participant: At any given point, he might accept the fact that there is more.

Gabriel: He might, or he might go through this earth-experience never accepting it, but when he gets to the other side, there is a grand and wondrous awakening!

Releasing and Prayer

Participant: Consciously we may say, "I really want to get rid of something!" but subconsciously our will is still hanging on. How can our conscious minds tell our will, "Hey, let go! I really want to get rid of this"?

Gabriel: Take all of these things that you perceive to be holding you back from your at-one-ment with God and make them a gift unto God. Ask the Holy Spirit to transform them into something wondrous. Take them to the Altar, as you perceive the Altar of God to be, and lay them there and say, "Here is my gift. I ask that it be transformed." The energy that is in anger or whatever, let it be transformed into a blessing and in its transformation it is gone! The Holy Spirit can do what angels cannot, for angels can only do the will of God and who is God?

You are. So, if your conscious mind says, "Get rid of this!" and your will says, "Don't you touch it!" the angels must abide by your will. But the Holy Spirit transcends all that. The Holy Spirit is the action of God and since you are God, and God is God — the unifying element here — the Holy Spirit in its transformation removes obstacles that angels do not touch. Have you not heard the saying, "Going where angels fear to tread"?

Participant: So when we ask for something, but it does not show up, it is the ego that is holding it back.

Then, we can ask the Holy Spirit to step in and take care of it.

Gabriel: Indeed. Now remember, most of you here are asking for physical things, for material things, not all of you but most of you. The material is the last plane to be affected. So if what you are asking for is a physical thing, you must go past that, up into the higher realms and ask for the realization of that which you desire to be made manifest. This relates to that part of the prayer, "The Kingdom on Earth, as it is in Heaven." You are bringing that realization into physical form. That in itself would remove your obstacles.

You never can have a blessing out here, externally, until you are aware of it in here, internally; for what is inside is the truth of you; what is out there is only the effect. What is outside of yourself is the effect, the result. When you are asking for something out there, you are asking for the effect to make the effect. All things come from the Father who is the source. You have to go to the source and allow it to be manifested on every level. Then it will out-picture here on the physical plane. This is where you perceive much time to pass between your asking and your getting.

So if you are desiring a physical, material thing, what is its spiritual basis? Let us say you want wealth; the spiritual basis of wealth would be abundance. If you wish to be successful, then the spiritual aspect of success would be your talent, which is limitless, and your ability, which is limitless. So you must go to the source. Prayer is very concise. I've come to the conclusion this day that it is not possible to put into words that which is formless.

Participant: We have an expression, "Putting the cart before the horse." And that's how I'm hearing what you are talking about. When we pray for something outside of ourselves, we are putting the cart before the horse. In prayer we are recognizing what drives us, who we are, and what we are. So, prayer comes first and everything else will follow.

Gabriel: Everything else will follow, indeed! Now, why didn't I think of that!

Participant: You did.

Gabriel: But that is what happens when you ask for things out there, you are approaching the God of out-there rather than the God within. Consequently you are asking the material for the material when you need to go to a higher aspect and find a spiritual connection and then bring it forth.

SECTION TWO

MEDITATION

CHAPTER EIGHT

WHAT IS MEDITATION?

You learned this morning how the Son of God connects to that sense of consciousness in which you become aware of your oneness with the Father. And now you will become aware of what true meditation is. As with prayer, there are many forms, many states of consciousness of meditation. There are no incorrect ways to meditate, but there are ways that are more successful in the purpose of meditation than others. It has been said on your earth plane that when you pray, you speak to God and when you meditate, you listen for God to speak to you. This is more or less correct.

Meditation is God Touching You

I told you this morning that when you pray, you are connecting with the Father, that pure resonance, that harmony. When you meditate, you become aware that, in that connectedness, there is something coming back to you. In prayer it is the child reaching to touch the Father in consciousness. In meditation you are aware the touching is being returned to you.

Since I have been channeling through Beloved Woman, I have become aware of the sensation of touch. I was not aware of touch before, but I have become aware of it, especially her face, what she wears upon it, and her garments. Touch is a most wondrous thing and it is very important in your world. One can say words and be misunderstood. One can look upon something and not perceive it in its truth, but when there is a touch, that you know. Your touching, how you touch, how you respond to touch, tells you much about yourself.

Those of you who do not like to be hugged are fearful that in the hugging you might be discovered to be less than what others think of you. So you turn away the hugs. But when you hug and are hugged back, there is an openness, an exchange of love that is free-flowing, welcomed, and not judged. And this is good!

It is this free-flowing exchange of love between you and God that is the purpose of meditation. It is for you to become aware of the touching back of God, the parent figure, in consciousness to you.

Concentration versus Meditation

Just as when you pray in lack, your answer comes in lack, it is also true that when you meditate and concentrate on a single thing, it is into that vibration that you are tuning.

For example, there are groups on your earth plane who teach meditation by staring into the flickering light of a candle. That is not meditation, that is concentration and there is a big difference.

Any meditation where you concentrate on a single thing is not meditation. It matters not whether it is the flickering light of a candle or a mantra or any single thing that holds your attention to it. You are only taking little steps into the truth of meditation. You are going as far as your mantra or as far as your candlelight will allow you, but you are not going past it.

Before you entered the earth plane — when you were still in your spiritual state of awareness — when you prayed to God, you knew that you had made a connection. When you meditated, you also knew that God had made a connection with you. Prayer and meditation are "two sides of a single page" or of a single coin, for one is the reaching to and the other is the receiving from. If you are taking your receiving only as far as a mantra, a candle flame, the heart of a rose, or whatever you use, you are not allowing yourself to be open to the Father's love and presence flooding back to you.

Some of you say, "But I must use something or I cannot meditate." That is because you have convinced yourselves of that. When you truly meditate, you are not seeking God nor are you seeking to entreat or ask God anything. You are being still and allowing the silence of you to bring forth from the Father that touch. It is your acceptance of it, of that touch, that is out-pictured in your meditation.

The Father does not need anything to become aware of you, for He is never unaware of you. But you perceive — in your level of evolution at this point — that you need something to make you aware of when the Father is touching you. That is all right and that is the purpose of meditation. Just as I told you this morning that the only purpose for prayer is to know God, so the only purpose of meditation is for you to know God knows you.

When you use a mantra, you are tuning in to a sound. It is a sound with limitations because you are concentrating on it. You are bringing all of your energies to a central point, which is the mantra. You are tuned in to that vibration and while it may bring you some "input," as you call it, it is not the pure channel that you are seeking. A true meditation connects you with that flow from the Higher down into that level which you perceive yourselves to be at, at this time.

Just as prayer transcends the limitation of the mind and of the emotions, so meditation quickens the mind into awareness of its totality, of its vastness, of its connectedness to God. Into the emotional body meditation brings perfect peace and love. Into the physical form it brings a harmonizing of the vibrations of the heartbeat, of the flow of blood, of the breathing, and so forth. Breathing is important in meditation for it prepares the physical aspect of you to receive the higher aspect of your Spirit.

I have told you before that only a minute particle of your Spirit dwells within your physical forms. There is enough of your Spirit to animate your bodies and to bring them into the awareness of life, but this minute particle is not the totality of you.

So when you meditate, what you are doing is bringing your awareness into that harmony that can be brought into the physical, emotional, and mental aspects of you. Just as prayer is lifting yourself to your higher aspect, so meditation is receiving — notice I did not say bringing down — that higher aspect that you connected into in your prayer.

To properly meditate one does not use candles, mantras, or sounds, for those will hold your attention to the physical world. While you will reach the higher vibrations of that physical world, you will not transcend it. To properly meditate you leave behind the physical, the emotional, and the mental. As a result of leaving those behind, you are then in receptivity of that pure essence of Spirit which gently comes forth and bathes you with its presence.

Meditation is the awakening of your awareness that God is present with you now, at this moment of your time. You become so totally aware of that Presence that you do not think of the position of your physical form. You do not have to bring your mind back from its wanderings, nor do you have to still your emotional voice that is telling you, "I am wounded. I am sorry. I am sorrowful," or anything of that kind. There is a bathing in that Presence that is totally consuming.

This would not necessarily bring any physical sensations. It does not necessarily bring a sense of euphoria or a mental state of enlightenment. However, it does bring to you the presence of God and in that all other things are included.

To meditate on a single thing is to cause that thing to reveal to you all of its secrets. Whatever you choose, be it a candlelight, a grain of rice as Buddha chose, a flower, it matters not; as you meditate on that single form, you are touching into that as your source and with that as your source, it will reveal all of its secrets to you. There was a man on the earth who did this with a peanut. It revealed to him all of its secrets and from that you got peanut butter! He learned how to milk a peanut!

Every inspiration that comes to you in meditation comes from the source of that inspiration. For example, if during your meditation the idea of a way of growing a better rose came into your mind, you can know that you have tuned in to that source — the vibration of flowers, of life proliferating — and you will know what to do to cultivate a better rose.

You can meditate on anything. If you have a question concerning something of a physical nature, such as a course you are taking, lessons you are learning, you can meditate on that and the answer will come to you because you have tuned in to the source of that knowledge.

Now there is nothing wrong with any of that, but in order to meditate for the purpose of making that connection with God, you have to recognize that God is the source of everything and not limit yourself to a particular vibrational rate, which happens more often than not with groups who meditate with music playing or who concentrate on a particular thing.

CHAPTER NINE

TRANSCENDENTAL MEDITATION

The purpose of transcendental meditation is never fully realized by its disciples because they get locked into the mantra. It is to the mantra that they are paying homage without their even knowing it. It is the mantra that is repeated over and over until finally it is the mantra they are being bathed in and that is the vibration that they take unto themselves. There is nothing wrong in that, but it is just extremely limiting. They concentrate on that vibration and therefore the energies are brought down into the physical. From those energies they are able to levitate and to move objects.

You have a question, Beloved Woman?

Participant: I was taught transcendental meditation which I have practiced for thirteen years. It was not a concentration meditation at all; it was the opposite. It was the lack of concentration. We were taught that the mantra floated in and floated out and so did our thoughts. But nothing was held; everything was allowed to pass.

Gabriel: That is true.

Participant: And when we felt there were no thoughts there, we would gently recall the mantra which would float back. But it was not concentration at all and it was not repetition.

Gabriel: It was not intended to be a concentration or repetitious. But the mantra was that key to which you were connected and this is my point: you connected into a key. Now, Beloved Woman, this is not a criticism. This is an explanation. When you take anything and you meditate on it, you are going to draw to you the energies thereof.

Now you must remember that transcendental meditation came from an Eastern mindset into a Western world where the mindset is totally opposite. So in order to span the gap there had to be a bridge and the mantra was that bridge. Now, there are gurus in India who practice transcendental meditation and who truly do transcend.

Participant: Okay. We felt we transcended.

Gabriel: Indeed. You did.

Participant: This, I guess, was our tool and we were told we were using the Sanskrit word for God. In other words, this word did not have meaning to us, just that it meant God.

Gabriel: It meant God. That was a sound they gave you. They never gave you a word. They gave you a sound. Is this not true?

Participant: No, it was a word.

78

Gabriel: But it was a meaningless word.

Participant: It had no meaning.

Gabriel: True. So therefore, it became a sound to you. Now when you get into a sound or into a flickering candle or anything, you are bringing in the bathing, the flowing of that element. You said your mantra drifted in and out and this is true. Your awareness of the candlelight or your rose petal or whatever will drift in and out, but you are bringing in only that energy. That is what you are being bathed in and this is where you will float. That energy takes you past the physical, but that is all it takes you past.

Let me explain. Western people do not think in terms that Eastern people think. Any meditation that comes from an Eastern mode of thinking and reaches into the Western mindset must have a bridge because of the difference in their thinking. It can appear that the Eastern races are rather hard-hearted and that they have little regard for physical life. It can appear that way, can it not? It also can appear that Western people are caught up only in physical things, acquiring possessions.

Would you say that either statement is a blanket truth about those people? Indeed not. But the way of the Eastern thought and the way of the Western thought are very, very different. Despite how they appear, Eastern people, from little ones up, are taught to think in spiritual terms. This is also some of their limitation, oddly enough. You would not think it would be so, but it is. This is one of the reasons for the caste system in India. It is because they are taught to think in terms of the spirit and they limit the spirit to the physical.

Native American people use their five senses in their meditations. They use incense, smoke, sounds, and sight. They meditate in such a manner that it encompasses the earth. There is nothing wrong with that, but they do not transcend the earth. They bring the spirituality to the earth and recognize it there, but they do not take themselves out of the earth. This is why in the days to come, the Native Americans of the old traditions will be the ones to teach you how to live on Mother Earth in perfect harmony. For centuries they have meditated on that and they know it well.

From your Eastern cultures comes a meditation that can teach you how to live while in the physical, almost without the physical. Buddha maintained his physical form on one grain of rice a day. Anybody here care to try that? So when you of one mindset enter into the mindset of another culture, there have to be some adjustments. Buddha would have found it difficult to explain to his disciples the holiness of Earth. But he could explain to them very well the traveling of the soul or the experience of the Spirit.

Your Native American cultures would find it very difficult to explain how to leave the earth and go past all of that into that which is. But they can tell you how to see the face of God in a buffalo. So you are dealing with different mindsets. This is why if you are of one culture and you try a meditation of another culture, it takes you awhile, because you have to transcend all the gaps in-between.

This is why when you meditate, do not use "tools," as it were — you do not need any of those things and it will not matter where you are — but rather go into that purity that is you. You will be bringing that purity into your awareness which is the purpose of your meditation.

Why do you think they teach meditation to warriors? They do, you know. Well, they did. I don't think your armies teach it now, but there was a time when every army on the earth learned to meditate. They knew how to meditate. The Ninja warriors of this day in your time are very good at meditation. This is how they transcend time, walk through walls, and do all the things they do. Do you know that the true forms of the martial arts are always based upon meditation?

Everyone knows that the power of the physical comes from the power of the mind and the power of the mind is realized best by someone who is used to leaving the physical and transcending everything that is limiting in their awareness — that is what meditation is for. It is to transcend your limitations and to recognize and allow into your awareness the limitlessness that you call God.

Back in the times when countries had more internal wars than external wars, where tribes or dynasties warred against each other, their power was not so much in how large their armies were. It was in their power of concentration and meditation of the men in those armies. A small army well tuned in meditation could conquer a large army who knew not meditation because the meditators knew how to concentrate their energies into a particular action.

In your country here, before the arrival of the Caucasian race, the natives had different kinds of warriors who did different kinds of things. They had messengers — runners, they were called — who would run from one tribe to another, often for a span of several days. When they meditated, they concentrated on speed and tirelessness and that was the source of their meditation. They also could cover a vast territory without water. They learned how to put a pebble in their mouths and from it recycle the very juices of their own physical form to keep them from becoming thirsty. That takes meditation!

In Africa they did the same thing. There are natives there who, even unto this day, can travel for days and days without water. It is because that ability became their meditation and the purpose of their meditation was to bring to them that element of strength that they needed to travel without water.

Those who are engaged in that activity called sports do a type of meditation, though they might not call it that. Have you ever watched a finely tuned athlete prepare for the challenge? Is there not as much mental preparation and emotional preparation as there is physical? What about a concert pianist? What about a poet? What about one who can sit down at a piano and bring into manifestation from the ethers, melodies that would touch your heart? What about the singer who can take a single song and by the way she sings it, bring tears to your eyes?

That is a form of meditation. It is a form of tuning in to the music and allowing it to come into them and be utilized. This is what meditation is. *It is bringing into your awareness a power beyond yourself and utilizing that power.* You can use it for anything.

Some of your most fearsome warriors were the most ardent meditators. It never occurred to them — as they practiced using their swords to lop off an ear, the tip of a nose, or the end of a finger before they killed their victims — that they were doing anything contrary or insulting to the power they had spent hours tuning in to. Some of your old Samurai warriors could slice bread so thin with their swords that you could read a book through it — and this was at 100 paces. They knew how to meditate!

Everyone has always thought that meditation had to do with God. However, meditation has been brought into so many avenues of consciousness that there are very few meditators upon the earth who truly do use it to touch into God. Even those whose intent is to touch God do not always touch into God. More often, if they do, it is by "accident," as it were, than by intent because there are so many avenues of expression of meditation and so many things to get caught up in.

Ninja warriors are good examples of those who use meditation for a specific purpose. You have ninja warriors upon your earth, here in this country, in this area. There is a great concentration of them here. They are able to appear as though they are not here. You had one of them sit through a whole day with you and not one of you was aware of him. No one knew he was here, but he was. In preparation for his visit here, the concentration of his meditation was for you to be unaware of him and thus you were unaware of him.

CHAPTER TEN

TRUE MEDITATION

What I will teach you this afternoon, you may use for anything you choose. We will get to the part of listening to God. But before we do, we have to get to the part of your listening to *you*, for that is the foundation on which you will build your ability to listen to God.

How many of you here feel that you truly know yourselves well? Now all of you know aspects of yourselves well, but none of you have ever tapped into the total aspects of yourselves because if you did, you would not be sitting here listening to me. You would have already tuned in to whatever you needed to know.

On many occasions I have said to you, "You already know everything," and everyone has looked at me very blankly. But you do know everything. The point is, you all have been rather lazy in your use of it. Because you have, it appears you have lost your ability to know, therefore you think you don't.

I would safely say that everyone in this room would like a better connection with the All-That-Is. Is that not true? You would all like to know that divine aspect of yourselves which is totally lovable, totally loved, and totally loving. I think that is a very fine place for you to start. When you are willing to go past the "selves" of you that you think you know so well and touch into that divine part of you, you will know the value of my words.

You all have a consciousness of the physical world and, indeed, you must because you dwell here. You all have a consciousness of lack — a large consciousness of lack. You all have a consciousness of illness and death. You have somewhat of a consciousness of love, somewhat of a consciousness of joy, somewhat of a consciousness of peace, and a small number of you have a consciousness of abundance. You have enough consciousness of these things to know these are what you desire.

How We Typically Meditate

For the most part, all of you here meditate every day on the negative aspects of yourselves. "Oh no I don't!" I can hear it ringing out through the room. "Not I! It isn't me! I bet it's the person behind me." The reason I say this is because when you sit down to meditate, one of the first things you do is get your bodies comfortable. That's all right, you have to do that. You can't sit uncomfortably and meditate.

So you get your bodies all comfortable, then you close your eyes and start your meditation using your mantras or whatever. You each have your own thing that you do and that's all right. But interspersed with all of that come the thoughts and feelings: "I think

I'd better shift the way I am sitting. Ah, that's better. I wonder if I unplugged the telephone? I think I did. Yes I did, I'm sure. Now, here we go. I know I forgot to do that. Oh, I'll have to do it later. Please let me remember to do that later. Yes, I will remember to do it later. Now, here we go again."

Shall I go on? Do you know what I am saying? Now I ask you, is that meditating? "Sort of," you say. And you are meditating on what? All the things that you should have done or should be doing or must do. "Now, I will get past all of that. I will settle down and I am going to meditate. Yes, I am! Now let me tighten my body and concentrate! Now, I'm not going to let anything disturb me. Well, maybe if I had a little music. I can't seem to get into it. Yes, a little music. Now I have it! Okay, now I am set. Uh, I better take off the foot appendages, the shoes. I have to take them off. I'll throw my legs under here, sit on them because so-and-so does that and he meditates well, so I'll do that. All right, here I go!"

In the meantime, your clock has been turning, and one of your eyes opens and looks at it and you think, "Fifteen minutes have gone by. I'd better stop now. I have to get dinner. I have to do this. I have to do that," and up you get. Someone asks you, "Ah, behold. What were you doing?" You respond, "I was meditating!" Sound familiar?

You also can add to this some incense, if you like, to tingle your nose and get the sinuses going. All of these things are your conscious attempts to do what you have already been doing unconsciously, subconsciously, for eons of time. You are concentrating on touching God.

Meditation is Stillness

Meditation is none of that which I have just described, none of it. When you meditate, you become aware of, release, and let go of anything that requires your energy. Your meditation is a time of receiving, not giving out. When you pray, you are reaching; that is an internal action. When you meditate, you are still. Remember, I taught you about action and repose. All of nature is action and repose, is it not? Everything has its time of doing and its time of not doing. The tide comes in and goes out. The sun rises and sets. The rains come and go.

Now prayer is lifting and tuning in to your higher self. Meditation is the repose of prayer. Every aspect of you becomes still and you rest in absolute peace in God. You do not busy your mind with a mantra; you do not busy your vision with a candle flame or a rose; you do not busy your emotional body by trying to feel love; you do not busy your physical form by becoming aware of a cramp in your foot or where your leg is; you do not busy yourself at all. You become the receptacle of all there is and that requires absolute stillness.

Absolute stillness is never acquired by concentration because concentration is an action. Stillness is acquired in only one way — relinquishing your fear. Every concentrated thing you think about is based upon fear: fear of failure, fear of your health, fear of not touching into God, fear of not meditating right, fear of not having a wondrous psychic experience, fear of not hearing the voice of God when He is talking, fear of whatever.

When you relinquish and let go of your fear, you are relaxing into a state where you are open, receptive, and willing to receive whatever comes to you. You know that whatever comes to you has to be of the highest and the best because its source is the Father and the Father never gives a stone when you have asked for bread.

How do you become still? How do you not hear the little voice that says, "Perhaps I didn't turn off the stove? I think I hear the cat outside and she wants to come in. What if, what if, what if?"

When you are still, you have no fear that you have or have not done something. You have no concern over the physical aspects of your body because you know it rests in perfect peace. Your mind does not chase about thoughts and drag them back to present them to you with the accusation of, "See what you've done!" or "See what you haven't done!" Your emotions do not twang at you with feelings of inadequacy or failure. Never brought to your remembrance is some slight that you did to a neighbor, some unworthy deed to a child.

None of these things enter your consciousness for you are resting in the totality of All-That-Is. And there you are being bathed in that endless love, that eternal wisdom, that unspeakable joy. You are not mindful of the clock for you know, in that receptive state, you are timeless. Time is only of the five senses.

You do not disturb yourself with the ideas of what you should be doing because you know that anything else you could be doing is simply an illusion and has no value. You do not compare your meditation with that of another person for you are keenly aware that what transpires between you and the Father is uniquely yours and is no part of anything else, for that is the one time you have His undivided attention. He is pouring out blessings unto you and this is your moment with Him. It is like the child who climbs upon the lap of Daddy at the end of the day when everyone else has gone to bed and enjoys those moments of the father's undivided love and comfort. That is meditation.

Meditation will bring to you more than what your

finite minds could comprehend for it will answer everything; it will soothe everything; it will love everything. It is not you loving, but you being loved; not you soothing, but you being soothed; not you comforting, but you being comforted; not you pondering, but you being fed. That is meditation.

Now, this takes practice for you are used to active meditation, are you not? You are and this is the most passive meditation there is. The key to it is your willingness to let go of your fears.

CHAPTER ELEVEN

THE POWER OF FEAR

How many of you here have decided that you want to keep your fears? Well, it takes a bit of practice because your fear isn't going to go down without a fight. After all, if it doesn't belong to you, it's an orphan. And once it becomes an orphan, the truth of it becomes known; its illusion becomes seen; and its deceptive powers are gone! Your fear cannot deceive you into thinking that you need it, so therefore, it is going to fight you.

I want to tell you a true story. Once there was a man who was falsely accused of a crime. He had no way of proving that he was innocent and he was put in prison for the rest of his life. He was a young man when this happened. Many, many years later when he was an old man, someone, on his or her deathbed, confessed to the crime for which he had been imprisoned. This confession freed him. They came to the prison, took this man, and said, "You are free and we apologize for the years you have lost." They turned him out into the world and gave him money, clothing, all sorts of things and they set him free.

The very next day he was pounding at the gates of the prison begging to be let in. They asked, "What are you doing back here? You are free after all this time and you are back here?" He said, "Please let me in!" They asked, "Why?" and he said, "Because it is too frightening out there! I have nothing to do! I have no one to tell me when to arise, when to eat, and when to go to bed. I have no one to tell me I'd better be careful or I'd better watch out for this-or-that. I am afraid out there for there is nothing to hold me!" And he pleaded to be allowed back into his prison.

In a way this is you. The idea of being without your fears is very frightening. It is ironic, isn't it, that you should be afraid to be free, but you are! Do you know what would be one of the first things you would be afraid of? "If I don't have any problems, what will I think about? What will I put my mind to if there is nothing to solve?"

Another thing you would say is, "If I am free to be totally lovable, what if somebody loves me? Oh, that is the most frightening of all! What if somebody loved me and in loving me finds out that I'm not what he thinks? What if someone gets to know me? Whatever shall I do? Far better that I be in the prison of fear where I am certainly safe from being loved. Lord knows, I'll have plenty to think about!"

Is it not more comfortable there than to let go of the fears that bind you and discover the rest of the rooms of your mansion? Is it not easier to lock yourselves in one little closet and decry the fact there are no bath facilities there rather than wander into another room where one might find them?

Letting go of your fears, beloveds, is the greatest challenge that you will ever meet for you have birthed them, nurtured them, fed them, and kept them well and happy lo these many years. They are your children. They are products of your creation. How could any parent slaughter his child or, more important, let the child go out into the dark and starve to death? What kind of a parent would you be? Well, I'm telling you a truth. If you desire to truly meditate and find that lovable self of you, then you must let go of your fears. You cannot drag the heaviness of them up into that state of consciousness that you must be in to be aware of the totality of God.

Is anybody here ready to let go of their fears now? On a conscious level indeed, but what about subconsciously? I could take each one of you — but I won't — and tell you what your real fears are, but they all come down to the same thing anyway, so I can tell you collectively. *You are afraid to see the glory of your own selves; you are afraid to be God.*

Because if you are God, Lord knows, you are responsible for yourselves, are you not? You can't play victim anymore. And certainly you can't punish yourself with illness and death. Most assuredly how are you going to point a finger at someone else and say, "That person has made me a victim"? You

95

can't. Who are you going to get angry with? Who are you going to be upset with? Who are you going to decry as unfair?

The hands are wondrous instruments. I have become aware of how wondrous they are indeed since I have used Beloved Woman's body. Your hands represent your ability to hold ideas, to grasp ideas, to allow these ideas to grow, and to open your hand and set them free to make a better world. Hands can also choke the life out of you. They can close over an idea and smother it.

I told you earlier how wonderful it was to touch, to be touched. But the same hands that can caress and bless, can also slap and slaughter. You have slapped and slaughtered yourselves all through the eons of time, beloveds. This is why you don't know how to meditate because letting go of your limitations is one of the greatest fears you have. You fear to allow yourselves to be you.

CHAPTER TWELVE

A MEDITATION EXERCISE

I will give you a meditation for you to use each day, as you choose. But I will tell you ahead of time, it will bring up your fears. It will cause them to knock on the door of your awareness and scream at you. You are going to think that everything that you have learned is a lie. You are going to think that this spiritual stuff is for the birds and that God is really out to get you. It is going to make you come into the awareness of your own divinity and that is so scary to you. On conscious levels, you crave it and on subconscious levels, you flee from it.

The most learned of people have glimpses of an eternal truth from time to time that strikes such fear in their hearts that they must disguise it, mutilate it, and present it in some unholy way. The results of that fear have been the religions that have been upon your earth for lo these eons of time. Anything that teaches you that God is separate from you and that you are not worthy to be called holy is a fear-based enemy that you have created to chase you around. Come out of the darkness, beloveds, and truly come into the Light of you.

When you meditate, I care not in what physical positions you put your bodies, do whatever is comfortable for you. You will instinctively do that which is right. Give yourselves credit for that. I ask that you use prayer as the foundation and that prayer is the one we discussed this morning: the reaching unto God and listening to the internal self of you for that clear bell-like sound that is your tone, your sound. There is no right or wrong, there is no success or failure. Even if you consciously do not think you have done it, you have by the very desire to do it.

As you have done that, allow yourselves to fall away from that center of Light. You may picture yourselves physically falling away from it; you can do anything you want. However, do not lock into any visualization you have; do not keep it as the only one; do not pronounce one better than another. Just allow the falling away, the falling away, the falling away of everything that comes into your mind and into your awareness because at this point everything that comes into your mind and awareness is going to be of your ego-self.

As you rise — and you will — you will notice that which falls away from you takes forms you have never seen before and you will realize that you are no longer visualizing, but rather the visualization is coming to you from "outside yourself," so it would appear.

You will go through that until finally you will come

to a state of clearness, an absolute clearness in which you are totally, completely, unaware of anything — your physical form, your thoughts, or your emotions. Nothing will matter to you. You will come into the sheer beingness of you without all the tapestry that you have added through the years. Do not try to hold this state of clearness. Allow it to come. Allow it to stay as long as it desires or for as a short time as it desires. It does not matter whether it is for a fraction of a second or a half-hour. Length of time is merely an illusion anyway. Do this every day.

Now I do not want anyone asking me for how long do I do this or how many times a day to do this, because if you have to ask me, you are not doing it right. You simply do it. Do not "do it until you get it right." You simply do it. At first, if nothing seems different to you, that is all right. Stay with it every day. As you do this meditation every day and as this falling away happens every day, you will finally get past the illusions and into the true falling away. You will get past what you think you are letting go, into what you really are letting go. You will go past the time when you think you have it into the time of really having it.

You will have some days when it will seem to you that you cannot meditate. That is all right. Then you will have other days when you seem to just "fall" into it, as it were. That is all right too. The important thing is to keep in mind that you are the open receptacle of the inflow of God-awareness. As you keep that in mind, the falling away will be a natural thing for the very inflow of that awareness will bathe away the illusion of fear. Fear and love cannot exist in the same place at the same time while you are pulling in that love.

I do not want you to envision how it should feel, how it should look, or how it should be. I want you just to allow it to happen. It is simple and it never fails. If you care to use your own meditation other times of the day for other purposes, please do. This meditation is for the purpose of your knowing that you are the receiver and God is the giver. It is your accepting the gift that is true meditation.

CHAPTER THIRTEEN

QUESTIONS ON MEDITATION

The Opening Prayer for Meditation

Participant: You said that we should use prayer as the foundation for meditation. Should we use the Lord's Prayer?

Gabriel: If you choose. Whatever you choose to use for prayer, feel it because prayer without feeling is empty words. If you choose to use the Lord's Prayer, that is well. It doesn't matter what prayer you use because after a while you will find there are no words; you are praying wordlessly. Then you have come to true prayer, just as you will come to true meditation.

The Falling Away in Meditation

Participant: You said that in meditation we should allow ourselves to fall away.

Gabriel: To release, let go, and allow the falling away, the falling away.

Participant: Are we supposed to fall away from the center of Light? That doesn't seem right.

Gabriel: You feel the center of Light and from it all other things fall away.

Participant: There is no action necessary on our part?

Gabriel: There is no action in meditation because then you are receiving. Your action is the prayer. The meditation is God's action.

Participant: If we really don't feel a sense of being raised, we can assume that it is happening anyway?

Gabriel: Indeed, you will be raised.

Falling From Negativity

Participant: As we meditate and picture these negative things falling away from us, you said there would be a feeling that there is a loss of something.

Gabriel: That is true. You will feel there is a loss.

Participant: Will that happen during meditation or sometime after the meditation?

Gabriel: It can happen at any point, Beloved Woman; it depends. Sometimes during the meditation you will think, "Oh, I feel as though something has gone from me that I love." Or perhaps a day or two later you will wake up in the morning feeling very depressed and not know why. You can know then that you have lost the negative aspect of it.

Participant: And praise God for those feelings because He has taken the negative thing away.

Gabriel: Yes, praise God because the beauty and the effect of the transformation will wait for you as a blessing.

Participant: As long as we don't grab it back again.

Gabriel: As long as you don't grab onto the negative aspect. The key is always to let the negativity go from you for it will be transformed into a blessing and the blessing will be returned to you to bless you.

* * * *

Participant: Gabriel, at another seminar you said that when fears show up, we could affirm, "I am in the garden of God, the presence of God." Should we do more than that to let negativity fall away?

Gabriel: Any of these things work, Beloved Woman. It depends on your state of mind. Sometimes it is easier for you to say, "I am in the garden of the beloved God," or it might be easier for you to affirm, "God is working through me now." It depends. All of it works. You just need to recognize the influx of the God power into your awareness. Remember, God's power is always present. But the idea of it "coming in" suits the consciousness of humankind at this time.

For example, you are all aware of an incoming new vibration to the Earth even though it is already here. People are becoming aware of it just now, so they think it is incoming, but it is already here. Because you have just become aware of it, you think it is brand-new. Just as with electricity, the cavemen had electricity, but they didn't know it, so it was not a manifested thing for them.

Active Meditations

Participant: Is it all right to sometimes actively do things in meditation such as is done in some guided meditations?

Gabriel: Oh yes, if you choose. A guided meditation that has you doing something is more concentration than meditation, but there is no harm in it

CHAPTER FOURTEEN

GENERAL QUESTIONS

Affirmations

Participant: Could you speak to us about where affirmations fit between prayer and meditation?

Gabriel: Indeed! An affirmation repeated, just words repeated, holds little benefit. But an affirmation that is truly felt is a proclamation of the blessings sought. In other words, whatever it is you desire, affirm you have it with great joy, "Ah indeed, I have this! This is wondrous indeed!"

One of the best ways to accept is to praise. Beloved Woman earlier said, "Praise the Lord!" She said it in jest, but she spoke a truth. When you praise the Lord God of your being, you are affirming His presence and you are rejoicing in it. So when you say, "Praise God!" or "Praise the Lord!" it is one of the greatest ways to receive, for it opens the channel and allows the blessings to come forth.

This is why many of the Christian Fundamentalists do a lot of praising. Without realizing it, they have locked into the concept of blessings. Have you not noticed how much they are blessed in their lives? Many of them are very blessed because they truly believe and they praise God. In their praising they bring the blessings forth. Now, their problem, as with everybody else, is fear.

The idea of praise and affirmation go hand in hand. When you affirm something, you are making it so. You affirm all the time because I hear your thoughts, "Well, I should have known I couldn't do that!" Or, "I should have known that he was going to that!" Now aren't those affirmations? They are indeed.

Now, what about swearing? Swearing is a form of affirmation in which you are affirming the most negative of conditions. Think about it the next time a curse word rushes to your lips. Try a blessing instead. When you affirm something, you are making it so. You are saying, "This is a truth and it will be!" So be mindful of what you affirm.

If you affirm you are going to have trouble getting to your job, you can be guaranteed you will. If you affirm the mode of transportation you purchased is going to give you problems, you can believe it will. If you affirm a person is going to give you a problem with something, he will. If you call someone stupid, he is going to react to you in stupid ways. If you affirm someone is grossly unfair, that is exactly what you will perceive and his actions will confirm it.

If you affirm, "There is nothing I cannot accomplish through the God in me," that is a great truth. If you affirm, "I know all I need to know about whatever I need to know about," that is a great truth. If you affirm, "God is preparing for me, here and now, a wondrous dwelling place that is my own to keep, to love, and to cherish," then it shall be so. But if you affirm, "I have no place to dwell," that is also so.

If you affirm, "I never have enough money to pay my perceived debts," then that is exactly what you will get. But if you affirm with great joy, "Indeed, I have abundance, more than enough to share!" that's exactly what you will have. If you affirm, "Love has gone from me," then it has. But if you affirm, "Love is ever present in my life and manifests to me in all forms," then so it shall. You can affirm anything you want because your will is done on Earth as you call forth your affirmation from the heaven world. Your will, beloveds, the Lord God of your being, that is "the Will" that will come forth.

Ascension

Participant: When I am ready to ascend from this life, I'd like to know how it works. Does the body just disappear?

Gabriel: The body slowly fades away. It disappears slowly. It becomes transparent and can be seen through until, finally, it is no longer visible. There is no "body," as it were, to take anywhere because you have taken it with you.

Participant: So my body is just gone. Is our medical world of today able to handle that?

Gabriel: Does it matter? The medical world would not understand it, Beloved Woman; that is a certainty. And if they could call your body back, as it were, they would dissect you to find out how you did that! But, other than that, do not concern your mind with it.

* * * *

Participant: I am a little confused about ascension. We don't pass over and then ascend? We would ascend right now?

Gabriel: Indeed. The actual ascending process takes about three days of your time to accomplish. But it has been done many times. Jesus was not the only one.

Participant: But to the eyes of the world, it appeared that Jesus did die.

Gabriel: It appeared that way to them.

Participant: But he wasn't really what we would call "dead" then?

Gabriel: Not in the sense of being lifeless, no, for he knew he had to take his physical form with him. Now, if he did not intend to take his body with him, he would have actually "died." But he allowed what you would term the "silver cord" to remain connected to his physical form. This is why Joseph took him into the tomb and did what he did. Joseph knew he had to prepare the body in a certain way so that the cord would not be severed.

Participant: In today's world, if he had been taken into the tomb and three days later they came back to get him and he wasn't there, they would have said, "Grave robbers."

Gabriel: Ah indeed. They did back then, as well. They accused the disciples of coming and taking away his body.

* * * *

Participant: Are there any documented cases, besides Jesus, of anyone else who has ascended?

Gabriel: Documented? Well, I don't know whether they are documented, but thousands of people have ascended. The Ascended Masters are a group of thousands—there are so many, Beloved Woman. I am not aware of any being documented because those who witnessed an ascension and who were non-believers decided to keep silent. And those who were believers, of course, they told everyone, but who believed them!

Death and Dying to the Old Ways

Participant: When you said, "You will think all this spiritual stuff is not good," it reminded me of something in the Bible where I think Paul said, "I die daily." Is that what he was talking about?

Gabriel: Indeed. When you "die" to old ways, it frequently becomes a matter of sorrow. You feel you have lost something that could never be replaced and your mourning is deep and sometimes long. That which you are dying to has been with you a very long time and you perceive it to be a part of you. It isn't, but you perceive it to be. When you sense that the old way is leaving you forever, you will mourn its absence. You will long to have it come back and you will perceive that you cannot be comforted unless it returns to you.

However, that is the illusion that is connected with death, for death is not a loss. You perceive it to be so, but it isn't. Death is the illusion given to transformation. When something or someone is transformed to a higher level, something has to be left behind and it is the leaving behind that ignites the feeling of grief.

You have spent eons creating the illusion of death. When that illusion dissolves, your fear becomes very great. "What will I do without death? How will I know how to be without it? What will become of me if I let something go?" What *will* become of you, beloveds? You step into Light and you become more! What you perceive you have lost is transformed into a glory that is set ahead of you on your path. You come unto this glory and you recognize it, not as that which you lost, but as that which you have found because it is without its illusion, its pain, its separation.

You never let go of anything that you love. It comes

around and stands before you to be embraced and loved, never as a thing of pain, but as a joy that you have not yet tasted. Every illusion that you have has a basic truth. Every sacrifice that you think you have made awaits you as a gift on your path to be presented to you in its truth — not as you thought you left it, but, in a joyous moment of recognition, you behold your creation in the beauty of it. Death is only the turning of a page, the turning of a wheel. That which leaves returns over and over again. Each time it returns, it is lifted up and it becomes more.

There are those of you here who have said to me, "You taught us that what we love becomes more. How can we believe that when sometimes what we love appears to go from us?" Beloveds, it is in the going from you that it is allowed to become more, so that when it awaits you on your path again, it is more than it was before. The love you feel was wrenched from you is given back a thousandfold.

Could the God of all good give you sorrow? Would He ask you to give up a beloved so that He might take him away from you? No. He polishes him up; He allows his light to shine; and He gives him back to you, more blessed than before, more lovable than before, more valuable than before. This is death, that's all it is. It is the transforming of that which can no longer serve into that which can.

Health and Maladies

Participant: Lately, I've talked to a few other people about our various maladies and everybody has a problem on their left side. Does that have any significance?

Gabriel: There is coming to your earth at this time (Editor's Note: Seminar was given November1991) a vibration that is of the female "density" — I will use that word. It is the "awakening," as it were, of the earth's receptivity of the higher realms, of the higher essences. When there is resistance to this, this vibration manifests in physical form, such as problems on the left side. When I say resistance, I do not mean it in a negative sense.

During all of the eons that you have been upon the earth, your spiritual progress has been so very, very slow until this last generation in which the spiritual progress has been accelerated. You have had things coming to your earth much more rapidly and more profoundly than you have had for eons before this acceleration. This is part of the "New Age," as you call it. So these vibrational rates are affecting humankind in ways they normally would not. Normally these changes would be so slow the effect would not be felt.

Because the vibration is more rapid, you are feeling it. If you will take note, everything of a receptive nature is being affected by the vibrations that are coming to the earth. Your electrical "grids," as you call them, are being affected. You will find during this year of your time that throughout your world, there will be outages of electrical power. Wherever there is a receiving aspect, the incoming vibrations affect it. There has to be that cleansing coming in.

This is why you are having trouble with things that conduct electricity such as water and electrical devices. Your problems are mostly manifesting now in the receptive aspects. These vibrations coming to the earth are disruptive at this point because the old, staid ways are being torn asunder.

These vibrations are affecting older people — people with older physical forms — more than the younger ones because the younger ones are more pliable and in tune with the new vibrations. Older people are more settled in their ways and this settled-in-ness is being disrupted. Therefore, they are getting pains in their appendages. All of this new vibrational energy is flowing through and, unless you hold it, it will pass. If you decide to hold fast to that which is disturbing you, it will remain.

Participant: How do we not hold onto that disturbance? People who have these maladies wake up every morning with the strained leg, arm, or elbow still there. How do we let go of the problem when it seems to be a part of our consciousness all of the time?

113

Gabriel: First of all, you have to recognize it is not a part of you. It is something that is passing through. As it passes through, you envision it going from you. A good thing to affirm, Beloved Woman, would be to say, "I am in tune with the changes that are upon the earth. I allow them to come; I allow them to manifest; and I allow them to pass. I do not hold them to me. I am a part of the flow of life."

Recognizing and Releasing Fear

Participant: Sometimes we'll be doing something and we see this fear. We know it is there and we see ourselves standing absolutely still before it. Is there anything that we can do to be rid of it or should we just let time pass?

Gabriel: Beloved Woman, how fortunate you are for you to see your fear. A fear you can see is easily vanquished. The moment that you see it and you feel yourself immobilized, rest in that. I have always taught you that there are action and repose. The action is, "Ah behold, I see a fear." And the repose happens while you are still, for then the Father can fill you with the courage and all the weaponry that you need to dispel the fear.

There is nothing wrong in being still when you behold a fear, for it is at that moment in your stillness that the Father can come and fill you with Himself. Then you can go forth knowing, "Ah behold, where is the fear?" It has fled before the

Light of Truth and there is no battle. Then you can look out with eyes of knowingness and you can say, "Ah behold, I have no enemies!"

* * * *

Participant: You talked about the fact that we all have unconscious fears, but we are working on these fears. A lot of us are meeting challenges and we are saying, "We don't like the way things are and we want them different."

Gabriel: Isn't it wondrous?

Participant: Well, it's a challenge, I tell you.

Gabriel: It is if you perceive it that way.

Participant: Well, yes, that's true, but how else are we supposed to perceive it? How else can it be but a challenge?

Gabriel: It is a challenge if you perceive it that way. Or you can perceive it as what it really is, a grand and wondrous learning adventure. Every circumstance that arises that you could perceive as a challenge, you could say, "Ah, how wondrous indeed! This is my opportunity to use what I have learned,"and exercise your spiritual muscles. You will find things change. It is when you lapse back into the old mode of limited thinking that it becomes a challenge.

Participant: Well, I know at one point I would say,

115

"This is the old way and I don't want this." But I'm not sure what I have to say to get rid of it?

Gabriel: You say to the old ways, "You are no longer a part of me. I welcome the new inflow of the Father that is me."

Participant: And just let it happen?

Gabriel: And let it be.

Participant: Ah, that's hard! Okay. Thank you.

Gabriel: One of the most difficult things for you to do is to let go of something because you perceive that you must always take action, take action, take action. Releasing and letting go is one of the most profound actions that you can take, and yet, it is the most difficult because you are always grabbing and hanging on.

There are some mothers who never let their children grow up. No matter if their sons are eighty-year-old men, the mothers still consider them "my little boy" even though they are hobbling down the street with their canes! Now it is the same thing, Beloved Woman, when you latch onto a limitation and hang onto it. No matter what circumstance comes to take it from you, you fight it off and you take it back, "It is my limitation and I will have it!"

Participant: When you say that, it is a frightening thing to me. I know I'm working on not having the fear, and now, you are telling me that it is happening on a subconscious level.

Gabriel: But Beloved Woman, the answer is simple. It lies in your trust that the Father gives you only what is good. You run into problems when you don't trust that divine source. When you feel you must do something, then the something you must do is to allow yourself to be open to receive.

That is the natural flow of life. As the answer comes to you, you become the disburser of the blessings, then more blessings come and you disburse, and more come and you disburse. You, by the very receiving of the blessings, become the action for them. But if you do not receive these blessings, how can you be the action for them? If you are busy scurrying about, the blessing cannot reach you.

For example, it is as if you are going to pour a cup of tea for someone. As you tip the pot, you move the cup over yonder, pour the tea all over the table, then curse it, and mop it up! But if you leave your cup there and allow the tea to go into it, then you can pass the cup as refreshment to others in the room. But if you feel your action part is to yank away the cup, it isn't the Father's fault if He's pouring out the blessings and your cup is elsewhere!

* * * *

Participant: When we prepare to do our prayer and meditation, my understanding of what you are saying is that our fears will come up more quickly for us.

Gabriel: They will fight for their life, indeed.

Participant: Do they mainly come up in terms of our relationships or from people we meet or situations we come into?

Gabriel: Your fears will manifest to you in any manner they can make themselves known because their purpose is to cause you to feel defeated.

Participant: If we come across an individual or a situation we did not expect and it seems challenging, or if a bill comes in for expenses we didn't think we owed, what is going on with that?

Gabriel: That is an example of your old fears manifesting themselves and saying, "See, I am still here, alive and well and you are in big trouble!" When you perceive you have a debt, you affirm, "Ah behold, here is an opportunity for me to be the channel through which abundance flows so that this bill is paid. I am only the instrument through which it flows. It has no part of me." Do not use the phrases "my bills" or "my debts" because then you are claiming them as your own and they will remain with you. But if you affirm, "This is a bill or debt that I am the instrument through which it is to be paid and then it goes from me," it will not remain with you. Remember that.

Angel of Destruction

Participant: I'm trying to get my understanding of the Angel of Destruction clarified. I thought we were to ask the Angel of Destruction to come and remove from us whatever belief we have that keeps us from knowing that we are God and the angel would help us remove our anger and whatever that anger was manifesting. But that hasn't happened for me. The manifestation of the anger has increased. Is the reason for the increased manifestation to help me see the anger within me and let it go?

Gabriel: Indeed! First of all, when you ask the Angel of Destruction to come, the angel cannot go contrary to your will. Verbally or consciously, you may have asked the Angel of Destruction to remove the barrier of anger. When the Angel of Destruction comes, some aspect of you is going to say, "Get your hands off that; it's mine!" The angel will simply withdraw. Never will an angel do battle with you over something.

If you ask for something to be removed, and subconsciously you are not ready to let it go, they honor you. They honor your desire to keep it. They will hover about and from time to time they will approach you. When you are ready to let the situation go, it is gone. But until you are ready to let it go, it will not go.

Significant Date - 11/11

Participant: People have been talking about 11/11 being a significant date. I thought it was November 11, 1991. I don't understand what that means?

Gabriel: That is another lesson. I don't care to get into it at this hour, but it is a vibration that is upon the earth that people are becoming aware of. They perceive it to be a door of sorts. Actually, it is the awakening of the consciousness of humankind to a higher level. The only door is that which they hold in their minds. There is no actual doorway, as it were.

Even one soul coming into that higher awareness brings all of humanity up. There are those who claim upon your earth that there has to be a certain number or the vibrational change will fail. Indeed not. There is one Christ in all and what happens to one happens to all. So if one person is lifted into the light of a better and higher awareness, indeed, all of humankind is lifted as well.

Do not limit yourselves by saying, "If this doesn't happen, that will fail." The Father does not regard things in that manner, nor does He perceive that there is one day of the week more blessed than another. That is your perception. Work with your internal selves to rid yourselves of the fear in your consciousness of limitation and you will find that all avenues are open for all of humankind to come up spiritually. But there are those who are of a certain vibration — and that is all right, that is where they are — who need to believe that they have to do this right now or else. That is the old fear mode pouring itself in to dilute the power of the spiritual aspect of it. That is all it is.

Participant: Aren't we lifting the consciousness now in doing our prayers and meditation?

Gabriel: Absolutely you are. But there are those upon the earth who would like to believe that there is a certain time and beyond that all is lost. Not so.

CLOSING PRAYER

I praise the Lord God of your being, and I ask that the Christ of you simply be in the fullness of that being, that you are transformed and lifted up into the Light that you are. For Father, I recognize You here, present, in this room, in these Thy children. I affirm that they also recognize Your presence in them.

I know that these words this day have touched and lifted and blessed and caused them to open wide the portals of their learning. And they are now, in this moment, transformed: in their consciousness into knowing-ness, in their emotional bodies into the feeling of Your love, and in their physical forms as perfect health. I know this, Father for I know You; and I know all that You are is the blessings that we treasure.

FURTHER INFORMATION

As indicated in the introduction, Gabriel presented over 250 spiritual lessons covering a wide spectrum of topics. All of these lessons are available for purchase as audiotapes and most of the shorter two hour sessions have been transcribed and put into booklets. Publication of the all day seminars in books is now underway.

For a complete listing of these lectures or if you would like further information regarding Gabriel's teachings and the continuing work of Rev. Penny Donovan, please contact:

Appleseeds Publishing
P.O. Box 101
Rosendale, NY 12472-0101
Phone: 845-331-8127
Email: appleseeds@hvc.rr.com

OR

The Gabriel Fellowship
P.O. Box 244
Rensselaer, NY 12144
518-286-3940
Web Site - www.gabrielfellowship.org
Email - info@gabrielfellowship.org